# The Shambles Of Science: Extracts From The Diary Of Two Students Of Physiology... - Primary Source Edition

Lizzy Lind-af-Hageby, Leisa Katherina Schartau

**Nabu Public Domain Reprints:**

You are holding a reproduction of an original work published before 1923 that is in the public domain in the United States of America, and possibly other countries. You may freely copy and distribute this work as no entity (individual or corporate) has a copyright on the body of the work. This book may contain prior copyright references, and library stamps (as most of these works were scanned from library copies). These have been scanned and retained as part of the historical artifact.

This book may have occasional imperfections such as missing or blurred pages, poor pictures, errant marks, etc. that were either part of the original artifact, or were introduced by the scanning process. We believe this work is culturally important, and despite the imperfections, have elected to bring it back into print as part of our continuing commitment to the preservation of printed works worldwide. We appreciate your understanding of the imperfections in the preservation process, and hope you enjoy this valuable book.

# SHAMBLES OF SCIENCE

BY

LIZZY LIND AF HAGEBY

AND

LEISA K. SCHARTAU

LONDON
ERNEST BELL
6, YORK STREET, COVENT GARDEN
1903

One Shilling. Net

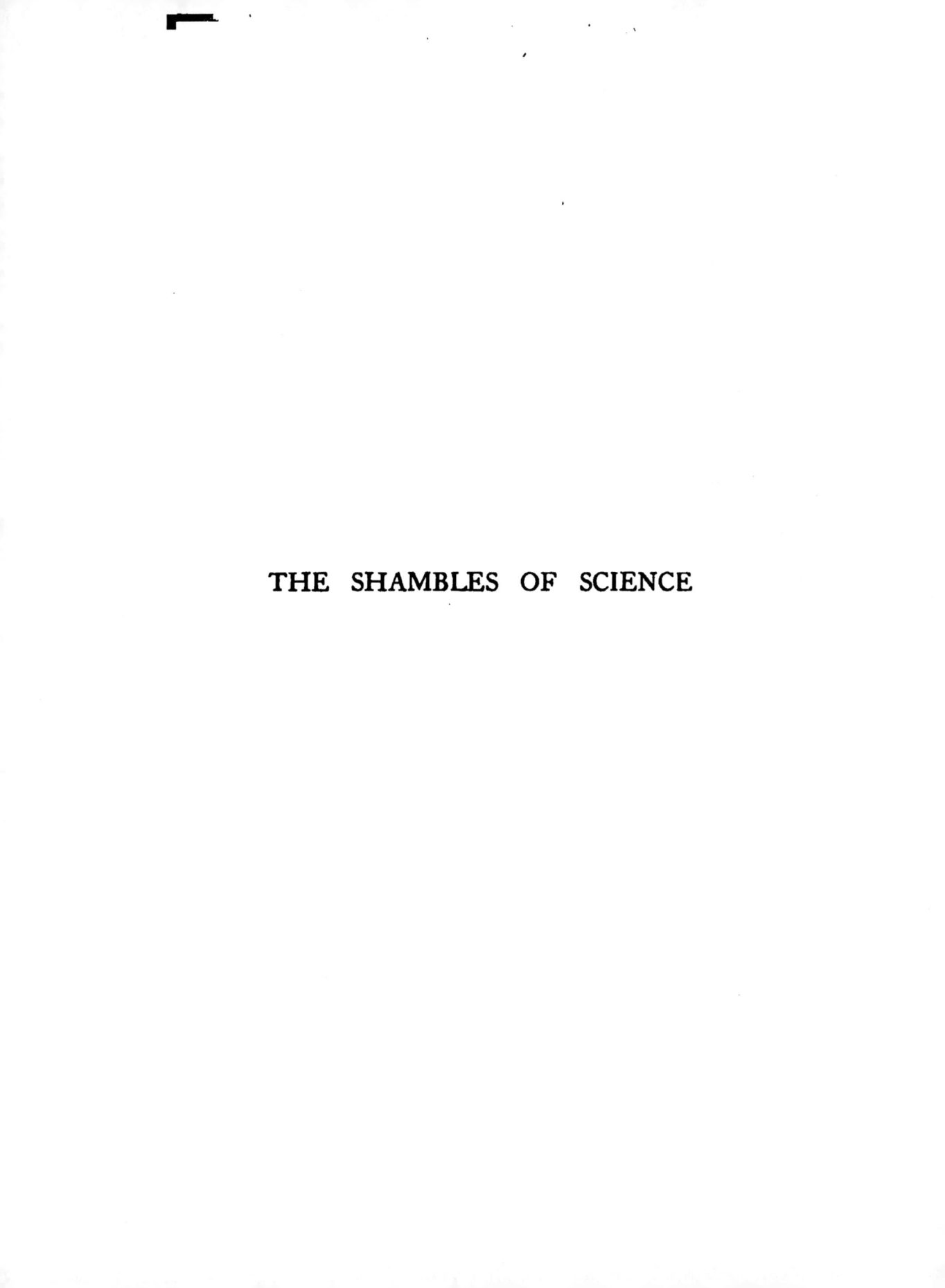

# THE SHAMBLES OF SCIENCE

# THE
# SHAMBLES OF SCIENCE

## EXTRACTS FROM THE DIARY OF TWO STUDENTS OF PHYSIOLOGY

BY

LIZZY LIND AF HAGEBY

AND

LEISA K. SCHARTAU

LONDON
ERNEST BELL
6, YORK STREET, COVENT GARDEN
1903

They are slaves who fear to speak
For the fallen and the weak;
They are slaves who will not choose
Hatred, scoffing, and abuse,
Rather than in silence shrink
From the truth they needs must think;
They are slaves who dare not be
In the right with two or three.

     JAMES RUSSELL LOWELL.

# Preface

# PREFACE

*"While I deeply respect the humane feelings of those who object to this class of enquiry, I assure them that, if they knew the truth, they would commend and not condemn them."* (From Lord Lister's Speech at Liverpool, October 8th, 1898.)

OUR object in taking up the study of physiology has been twofold: first, to investigate the *modus operandi* of experiments on animals, and then to study deeply the principles and theories which underlie modern physiology.

The two are closely related, for the rapid strides on the way of progress, which physiology claims to have made within the last fifty years, have passed over the bodies of uncountable long-suffering animals.

We are all familiar with the again and again repeated description of the pain involved in experiments on animals as being similar to that caused by a prick of a pin. Words like the above-quoted imply that anti-vivisectionists do not know the truth about vivisection, and that, if they did, they would at once give up their ill-informed agitation, and replace it by a profound admiration for the great men who are engaged in this praiseworthy and unselfish practice.

The contrast between the accounts of the cruelty of vivisectional experiments given by vivisectors and by the opponents of the system is indeed great. We have in vain sought for "the truth" that should change our views in textbooks, treatises, journals in German, French, and English, where experimenters themselves describe their work. Our study of the experimental literature did not teach us that anti-vivisectionists are mistaken, but, on the contrary, confirmed the justice of the accusations made by them. Was Lord Lister's truth only to be found within the walls of the laboratories? It was not altogether impossible that humbler vivisectors than Lord Lister, when describing their experiments in books and papers, are too shy to dwell on their own tenderness and consideration for the animals, and that they prefer to let the reader guess the indescribable and secret kindness which dominates all their doings.

And so we decided to find out the truth practically. This would also give us the best opportunity to listen to the materialistic and non-moral theories that dominate experimental physiology, as they are proclaimed by some of the foremost experimenters of to-day.

Modern science is infatuated with the glory of its own success, and it too often forgets that verbal classification and nomination are not always explanation. The intellect has become the sovereign to which everybody bows, and this self-adoring ruler hates to acknowledge the dominions of the heart, the soul, and the spirit, over which he has no power. At no time has a new criticism of the limits of pure reason been more imperatively needed. Physiology is soaring high up in the air like a proud bird of prey. But it carries nothing but the mutilated bodies of weaker and less cruel creatures; the spirit of life which it tried to catch was too subtle for its murderous fangs.

We desired to study how physiology is taught without and with vivisection. We became partial students of the London School of Medicine for Women, where vivisection is not allowed, and we attended the lectures on physiology there. We then sought and obtained permission to attend various courses of lectures on advanced physiology, and also demonstrations, numbering some fifty together, at other laboratories in London.

We have given our full names and addresses and paid our fees. Whenever medical students have spoken to us about vivisection, we have made no secret of our opinions. If anybody had cared to enquire, our connection with the Scandinavian Anti-Vivisection movement could easily have been found out. Our studies in physiology, however, have been entirely private, and carried out independently of any society.

It was not at first our intention to make our experiences public in this way; we only hoped to be able to do our work better with them. The idea of working for a final examination and scientific degree, which we at first held, has been given up, because physiology is at present inseparable from experiments on animals, and nobody objecting to them could have any chance of obtaining a degree.

We now think that some of the things

we have heard and seen in England may be of interest to English anti-vivisectionists, and we have therefore decided to compile part of our notes and reflections and to publish them.

Vivisectors are extremely anxious to spread their ideas among the young students, and they are not in the least ashamed of their teachings. They ought, therefore, not to object to these comments on their doctrine by two *very* attentive pupils. The names of the lecturers and demonstrators have been omitted in the accounts of the experiments, as this is not meant to be a personal attack, but an indictment against the system.

The importance of personal experience of the methods of vivisection for those who throw themselves heart and soul into the battle against it cannot be exaggerated. We hope that more and more ardent friends of this cause of mercy will enter the laboratories, see the deeds of darkness tolerated in Christian countries, and tell the world what they have seen.

To fight against vivisection is to fight against the principal fortress of the foe of idealism and spiritual evolution.

Not until this fortress lies shattered, and even its ruins are removed from the face of this earth, can we justly claim to possess civilisation.

*April*, 1903.
LONDON: 32, ST. ANN'S TERRACE,
REGENT'S PARK, N.W.

# CONTENTS

|  | PAGE |
|---|---|
| THE DEATH OF VITALISM | 3 |
| "PAINLESS EXPERIMENTS" | 11 |
| FUN | 19 |
| AN EXPERIMENTAL PRODUCTION OF BLOOD-CLOTTING BY INJECTION OF A NUCLEO-PROTEID | 29 |
| THE QUIET CAT | 37 |
| SCARCELY ANY ANÆSTHETIC | 45 |
| AN EXPERIMENT THAT "IS NOT SUPPOSED TO BE USEFUL" | 55 |
| THE DOG THAT ESCAPED | 67 |
| A DOG INJECTED WITH A SUBSTANCE DERIVED FROM A LUNATIC | 75 |
| MORE EXPERIMENTS | 85 |
| A TROUBLESOME DOG | 91 |
| PAIN | 101 |

## Contents

|   | PAGE |
|---|---|
| THE STRUGGLING CAT | 109 |
| LONG EXPERIMENTS; OR, THE FATIGUE THAT CANNOT BE DEMONSTRATED | 117 |
| THE ONLY COMPLETELY SATISFACTORY METHOD | 129 |
| A GRAND DEMONSTRATION | 139 |
| VIVISECTION BANKRUPT | 151 |
| ANÆSTHESIA | 159 |
| FROGOLOGY | 167 |
| THE SCHOOL OF MERCILESSNESS | 183 |
| AN EXACT SCIENCE | 191 |
| WHERE DO THE ANIMALS COME FROM? | 197 |
| THE BARREN TREE | 203 |

# The Death of Vitalism

# THE DEATH OF VITALISM

Armed with scalpel, microscope, and test-tube, the modern physiologist attacks the problems of life. He is sure that he will succeed in wrenching the jealously-guarded secrets of the vital laws from the bosom of Nature.

Old-fashioned physiologists were not so afraid of admitting that in their studies of the functions of the living body they often had to turn away from problems which cannot be solved by the experimental method.

But the "reverent study of Nature" is ridiculous to the physiologists of to-day. The "animal machines" are as yet somewhat intricate, and the laws that govern these machines are not so exact as the physiologists would like, but still they are confident that one day they will have penetrated the depths of the phenomena of life. They only want millions more of animals to experiment upon, better knives, better operation-holders, more powerful microscopes, finer electrical batteries, and they are sure the victory will be theirs. They may even cherish the secret hope that one day a real Frankenstein will arise from among the ranks of prominent physiologists.

In the Croonian Lectures for 1901 Professor Halliburton says:

"We sometimes speak of physiology as the application of the laws of chemistry and physics to life. Since this conception of the aim and object of physiology has pervaded its disciples, the progress of physiological knowledge has been rapid and fruitful.

"When Helmholtz, Ludwig, and their contemporaries set themselves to rescue our science from the slough of mysticism, they placed it on a firm basis and no doubt hoped in time to be able to expunge the word 'vital' from their vocabulary. But all must admit that that time has not yet arrived.

The neo-vitalists, it is true, have not the same contented and reverent frame of mind in relation to the meaning of the word 'vital' as the older vitalists had. They admit its unsatisfactory and *unscientific* nature; they use it merely as a convenient expression for what *cannot at present be brought into line with the forces that operate in the inorganic world*,[1] and not merely as a cloak for their ignorance. The use of this word becomes most frequent when we have to deal with mental phenomena, and the question for the future is whether the manifestations of vitality are only physical and chemical after all, or *whether there is really some other and at present unknown force, or unknown aspect of known forces*,[2] which in the meanwhile we must be content to label as vital.

"On such a fundamental question as this there is obviously much room for differences of opinion. The answer is certainly in the region of the unknown; some may place it with du Bois-Raymond in the region of

---

[1] Italics ours.　　[2] *Ibid.*

the unknowable. That may be so; one hopes that it is not, for if we once admit that any subject is unknowable, we place an impenetrable bar upon research, and remove any stimulus to investigate it afresh."

The new school which regards physiology simply as a sort of physico-chemistry is indeed quite free from "the slough of mysticism." In emancipating themselves from the old vitalistic and reverent views, the adherents of this school have also expunged the unscientific and misty attributes of mercy and kindness towards inferior creatures which are coveted by less advanced men.

The result of all their experiments is a philosophical retrogression; they have returned to the theory of Descartes, and reduce animal life to a kind of machinery, the springs and screws and wheels of which will be revealed by their latest improved instruments. They seem to be especially influenced by the Cartesian doctrine, that animals possess neither feelings nor consciousness.

The "exact experimental analysis of physiological phenomena" cannot be concerned with feeling, and the mechanical explanation of life is quite free from religious superstition.

A host of disbelievers in experiments on living animals as being the means of true physiological knowledge held the vitalistic views. Among them, the famous naturalist Cuvier deprecated the method of physiological research which is now accepted by physiologists of the twentieth century as being the only reliable one.

Vitalism stands in the way of "the rapid and fruitful progress" of vivisection, materialism, and atheism, and therefore vitalism has to be killed.

Experimental physiology is triumphant over its new faith, which places the phenomena exhibited by living and non-living matter equally within range of its physical and chemical apparatus.

To tear living beings to pieces, to analyse the properties of the warm blood that spurts out from lacerated vessels, to mince the twitching muscle and squeeze its fluids for the test-tube, to cut vibrating nerves, to bring disorder and disharmony into the perfectly united parts of the living body, are now the highest forms of this science.

It is only natural that scientists who investigate the living organism in this way find nothing that is alive as it was. They measure the physical and chemical manifestations of their material; they do not recognise the vital—they have no instruments with which they can pick up that; and, besides, every physiologist of rank in these days despises the idea of a mystical something which does not make obeisance to his genius.

The skilled mechanician is master of the laws which he thoroughly understands; the experimental physiologist is master of Destruction, but he is mastered by Creation.

It is indeed paradoxical to worship a physiology deprived of "vitalism"; the results of such a science are also paradoxical and dead.

"Painless Experiments"

*Physiological Laboratory, University of London
Imperial Institute*

DECEMBER 2ND, 1902

## SCARCELY ANY ANÆSTHETIC

THE tools of the experimental physiologist are many. The simple scalpels, scissors, forceps, pincers, knives, hooks and saws, with their concomitants of cotton wool, sponges, threads of silk, vaseline, etc., which are spread in rows on the glass slabs in front of us, are only some of the cheapest and simplest requisites of the humble artisan in the trade of vivisection. Nor do the various forms of animal holders, operation-tables, and boards with different kinds of head-holders finish the equipment of even " un petit vivisectorium." Much labour, thought, and study are devoted to the improvement and invention of these, and scores of workmen in the great centres of our Western civilisation are employed in the manufacture of apparatus for holding live animals, but all the same, they are only the most elemental necessaries of everybody who the diminution. The vagus stimulation is made stronger and longer, and there is a bigger fall in blood-pressure and more marked diminution of the kidney.

The animal's head is covered with a cloth, and there are layers of cotton wool over the exposed viscera to prevent them from cooling. There is a faint whining sound which we first think comes from some other dog operated upon in another room. But the whining grows louder and more piteous, and the animal struggles so that the cotton wool moves to and fro. The assistant demonstrator pours a few drops of something on a cloth over the head, and the lecturer tells us that the animal has had morphia and a little chloroform. We do not doubt that it must have been very little of both. The animal is quiet for a minute or two. Supra-renal extract is injected into the jugular vein; the writing points of the levers now run into one another and cause disorder in the tracings. The dog begins to whine and struggle again whilst the demonstrators are engaged in rearranging the levers. Their ears, however, are not trained to listen to that kind of sound, and five minutes elapse before they notice anything. A few drops of the contents in the bottle of something are again applied to the cloth.

The first rise in blood-pressure and increased kidney volume after the injection of the supra-renal extract are studied, then the constriction produced by the kidney vessels. The vagi are now cut to let us see the effect on the volume of the kidney, but the lever which shall demonstrate this does not make any movement. Something has gone wrong. The volume pulse has disappeared. "This does not teach us much about the great flow of blood through the kidney," says the lecturer, and adds, "We cannot tell whether there is an increased or decreased flow of blood through it."

It is very important for the success of these experiments that the oncometers be perfectly air-tight. There is a leak now, and the oncometer has to be reopened and the packing of the strips of wool and vaseline mixture round the kidney must be done again. It takes some time, and the cries and struggles of the dog grow louder and more forcible. The lecturer looks a little nervous now when, even with good will, it is impossible not to hear and see. The trusted bottle of something is again called to the rescue; the situation is rather awkward.

The renal vein is compressed by means of a piece of wire and a rubber ball: there is a slow rise in blood-pressure. The clamping is repeated longer, and now there is a fairly considerable rise in the volume of the kidney.

It would be a great pity to miss another dose of supra-renal: comparison is the essence of the wisdom of life. We have now tried clamping without supra-renal. *What would be the result of clamping after supra-renal?* A dose is injected. Whilst the constriction is still present, the golden opportunity is grasped, and the vein clamped.

Be prepared to listen: *the rate of rise is this time quite slow.*

A solution of sodium sulphate is injected, some amusing things are said, and most of the spectators laugh. The injection produces a slight rise in blood-pressure and a gradual and very slow dilatation of the kidney vessels. The dog groans as loudly as he can with his tied muzzle. He must have managed to loosen the strings, for now the low whine has grown into a suppressed and long-drawn howling; sometimes it is like the stifled sobbing of a little child; once or twice there is a distinct bark. The lecturer looks vexed, and the bottle of something is again exhibited.

What are the watery and smell-less contents of this bottle? We are quite sure that the lecturer is no great friend of deep anæsthesia, for in the book which he recommends for the use of students, the readers are several times warned against this. Where the stimulation of the superior laryngeal is taught, we read: "In this instance, and indeed for all these nerve stimulations, the rabbit must not be too deeply under the anæsthetic." Again, in treating of the stimulation of the central end of the vagus, we noted the following sentence: "This result is much better obtained if the anæsthesia is not too deep." From another part, treating of the stimulation of the sciatic nerve, we quote: "Often, too, struggling movements are produced, especially if the animal be only lightly under the anæsthetic, when with each convulsion the blood-pressure rises considerably. The only completely satisfactory method of obtaining a pure pressor effect is to previously curarise the animal."

The lecturer is now, of course, only using light anæsthesia, and he has not to-day cared for the "only completely satisfactory method."

After another injection of sodium sulphate and some more clamping of the renal vein, a cannula is tied into the ureter to show the effect of the diuretic. The lecturer finishes by saying he is afraid that the volume-changes which have appeared are not at all reliable, and that the experiment has not been altogether a success. "The apparatus for kidney work is not so good in this place, for we work on other organs here; but of course it is the method that it is important to learn."

Yes; it is the method, the atrocious method of the vivisectors, that it is important to learn.

After the lecture we examined the dog closely, and were shown the details of the kidney and clamping apparatus. As we bent down over the quivering frame of the tortured animal, it *growled* repeatedly. Who can stand by the side of a helpless creature thus tormented without being filled with a burning indignation against the perpetrators of such deeds? Only he who cares no longer for the things that make life worth living—only he who has lost the sense of shame at cowardice, which is the never-failing sign of every soul that has attained to true culture.

We had the satisfaction of speaking to a

medical student who expressed disgust at such demonstrations.

When we left, after an hour and a quarter, the dog was still growling and whining on the operation-table.

# Pain

# PAIN

Through the noise of the machines, the buzz of the electrical batteries that stimulate, the whistle of the air pumped into cut throats, through the talking and laughing of men bent over their victims, there comes the cry of pain.

Behind the light clouds of smoke from cigarettes, consumed in ease and comfort, from among a mass of delicate machinery, of metal and glass and caoutchouc, of skin slit up and quivering entrails drawn out from the writhing mass of flesh and bone and nerve, there are eyes that gaze out in anguish, eyes from which the hope of death has fled.

Nobody hears the cries, nobody heeds the looks.

"Pain?—there is no pain in our laboratories," they would answer if you asked them, and add: "*We* have never seen an animal in pain."

No, it is true, they do not hear and they do not see, for their ears have been stopped and their eyes blinded by the Deity of Selfishness, whose servants they are. Pity has fled from their temples long ago, and if she tried to enter again she could not breathe the stifling air. They have left off sentiment long ago; they do not think of the possibility that animals, nay, *animal machines*, ever feel pain. And when an animal screams or struggles too much, a faint suggestion that others might mind—because others are ignorant—may enter their brains; but "we have never seen an animal in pain"—and we are not going to see it either.

Do you think this moaning dog, with his spleen in a glass box, feels anything? You do; well, that is just an instance of how laymen misunderstand everything. My dear sir, you know nothing about reflexes, so, please, don't come and teach us anything.

Many are quite honest, as honest as the

deaf and blind man who swore that no thief had passed the place where he stood.

There are some who are half-conscious of the fact that pain inflicted on animals is pain; they talk much about anæsthetics and use a little. They have read what a lot of people, who are not altogether insane, say about the cruelty of vivisection, and they are above all anxious to show how humane they are.

There are others, but only very few, who admit that pain is inflicted, and who openly declare that they have the right to give any amount of pain to the lower animals, if thus they can gain knowledge or prolong the lives of men.

But on the whole vivisectors appear perfectly unconscious of their infliction of pain, and this is the chief form of complete unconsciousness that at present is manifested within the physiological laboratories.

The chemist and the physicist do not take the tastes of their material into consideration, and the physiologist, who feels more and more sure that life is nothing but the result of an aggregate of chemical and physical laws, does not enquire into the feelings of the centre of such laws on which he is working, whether it be a frog, a rabbit, a cat, or a dog. All animals are research beasts.

Once we saw a physiologist engaged in a long and painful experiment on a dog. A few days before a little child had been born to him. He belongs to that class of experimenters who appear to be in a state of perpetual moral anæsthesia in their feelings of the relationship to the animal world.

As we watched the work of his merciless hands we thought of the newborn babe that lay waiting for the father's tenderness. When his day's labour was ended, he would no doubt go home and rejoice over that little child, and his heart would respond to the cries from that tiny throat and his eyes would not be blind to the signs of pain in that delicate body.

He would scorn a parallel drawn between the helpless dog and the helpless babe, and he would be at a loss to find words strong enough to express his disgust if a very advanced colleague advised him to test the same experiment on his own child.

Times have changed, and the sympathy for the sufferings of "the little ones" in this world of struggle and pain has in some souls been extended to include also the animals. They cannot think as we do or speak as we do, but they can feel and suffer and be faithful unto death.

The vivisector has not yet had time to study these new ideas.

But there is a very old word which he has listened to many times—at least, when he too was a little child—and that is:

*Blessed are the merciful, for they shall obtain mercy.*

# The Struggling Cat

MARCH 9TH, 1903

*University College*

## THE STRUGGLING CAT

In a former lecture on the production of heat in glands the lecturer said that he was sorry he could not make a certain experiment of Heidenhain's, which he thought was a very uncertain one but still worth repeating. "We are rather short of dogs now in the laboratory, so I could not have one for this afternoon," he said. The laboratory resounded with howling and barking of dogs when the lecturer said this, but all those dogs were perhaps destined for the knives of other scientists, and the accidental waste of laboratory material, of which he was the involuntary cause at his last lecture, may have left him without material for this one.

Once he had to manage without an animal,

but to-day he need not feel uncomfortable for he has got a cat.

When we enter, ten minutes before the lecture is going to begin, there is a tabby cat with neck cut open struggling violently on an operation-board put in a corner of the room. Some students are already there, and among them there are a few exceptionally thoughtful. One looks quite upset when seeing the animal, and turns to the others, saying, "I am sure they have forgotten to give the cat an anæsthetic. Do tell the lecturer." A young man walks out of the room to let him know that they have forgotten to anæsthetise the cat. The lecturer enters, smoking his pipe, looks at the cat, tightens the strings that hold the legs—and walks out again. The humane student, a girl with a delicate and refined face, looks sad and anxious. She tries not to look at the animal, opens a book and pretends to read. She does not like to be called sentimental, and she supposes that it is necessary for science to do these things, but still she cannot help crying when she looks up and sees poor pussy in this state. "Oh, it cannot be suffering much," she says with tears in her eyes; "they cannot have done anything to it yet, can they?"

She then puts her fingers into her ears and tries only to think of the contents of the book. Another lady, who works to obtain honours in physiology, enters the lecture-room. She comes from the laboratories and sits down by the side of the sensitive girl, who at once asks her something which is answered by a laugh. The aspirant to physiological honours must think the other very foolish.

The cat struggles on his rack as before. There is a small group of women students who have just entered, and who discuss the cruelty in an experiment like this where it is clear to everybody that the animal is not under anæsthesia. Two of them express indignation at what they see, the others make light of it.

The lecturer begins by telling his audience that he has been working with this cat earlier in the afternoon. (The humane girl in front of us starts.) He has been repeating Heidenhain's experiment with exciting the sympathetic in order to study the increase in the production of heat in the submaxillary gland, but he has not been able to produce the desired effect. He wishes now to repeat it again to us, to let us also see that there is no effect. He then starts the stimulation and nobody notices any effect, except the cat, who in vain tries to be spared.

When the non-effect is satisfactorily demonstrated, the lecturer rings the bell and tells the servant who enters to take away the cat.

For how many hours had that cat been stretched on the operation-board, with open wounds and electrodes on quivering nerves, and for how long a time still would it be left in that position?

During four demonstrations in this lecture-room nothing has been said indicating that any of the animals have been anæsthetised. We have not seen any anæsthetic or narcotic used, and the conditions of these four animals make it clear to us that they were not under anæsthesia.

*Once* the lecturer told us that he had injected curare.

The quiet cat and the quiet dog were allowed to remain till the end of the lecture; the struggling cat and the struggling dog were taken out before the hour was over.

Comment is needless.

# Long Experiments

*Physiological Laboratory, University of London
Imperial Institute*

MARCH 12TH, 1903

# THE ONLY COMPLETELY SATISFACTORY METHOD

This time the lecturer has made up his mind not to have any disturbances like those caused by the troublesome dog during a former lecture, and he has doubtlessly found the remedy to be curare. For the big white bull terrier that is fastened on its back to the operation-table, mangled and mutilated in a way that according to the laws of Nature would be incompatible with any life left, does not make a sound or a movement. The chest has been transformed into a deep and broad red hole, skin, muscles, ribs removed, the lungs and the heart exposed, the neck opened, a tube tied into the trachea, and artificial respiration is being kept up.

The subject of the lecture and demonstration is the total blood-pressure variations, and there are not less than four records taken of the differences in pressure in the carotid artery, pulmonary artery, and in the left and the right side of the heart.

An hour is spent in the study of these variations and the tracings obtained are supposed to be extremely correct, exact, and typical. Instead of the mercury manometer Hürthle's rubber manometer is used. There is a great inertia in the moving parts of the mercury manometer, because the pressure variations can only be recorded some time after they have taken place, and it cannot record the highest and the lowest pressures when changes occur quickly.

The rubber manometer is supposed to possess "the least possible inertia," but in time it will surely be found out that this one also possesses a good deal of inertia. Supposing all the minute alterations and delicate changes in the flow of blood in the living animal could be correctly described by the levers scratching lines on the sooty paper, we still could never, by methods like the one used now, learn to know the *normal* flow of blood.

This half-flayed, paralysed dog, with hundreds of small blood-vessels cut and bleeding, with pieces of glass forced into opened veins and arteries, with the heart and lungs unprotected from the influence of the air and light in the room, is he now in a normal state, and can we trust even a rubber manometer with the least possible inertia to tell us how his blood circulated, when, some time before, he was a happy and healthy dog, running by his master's side, and wagging his tail in response to the kind words from his human friend?

The inconsistency in experimental physiology must strike every thinking person. In normal respiration there is a rise in blood-pressure during inspiration and a fall during expiration. Every budding vivisector knows that *artificial respiration entirely reverses this*, and that the inflation of the lungs produces a fall of pressure, whilst there is a rise in expiration. In artificial respiration blood-pressure is thus entirely *abnormal*, and nothing of any value whatever for the knowledge of the normal flow of blood can be gained by this method.

And yet "the records" of the blood-pressure in this animal are received as deeply scientific and important information. If the pump were stopped and no more air forced into his throat, his lungs would collapse, and the dog would die, for death is the only normal result of such a bodily state, and Nature is a great deal more merciful than Science. But physiologists care little for the laws of Nature, and are brimming over with pride in their knowledge of the blood-pressure. That this knowledge to a very great extent is based on experiments on creatures mutilated nearly to death, kept artificially alive with an entirely abnormal circulation, matters little to them.

In the physiological laboratories endowed by public generosity for research believed to benefit the impaired health of humanity, or to ennoble the minds of men by laying the rich fruits of true knowledge before the intellectually hungry, thousands of dogs are treated like this one, and absurdities, that pass under the heading of physiology, are sent out into the world and received with bows and reverent gratitude by the great public, who think that some one wiser than they will find the philosopher's stone under the veils of scientific terminology, which they cannot penetrate.

There are some who have sought earnestly and patiently, and found nothing but words— only words; but behind them they have seen the only reality hidden from public view— the immeasurable burden of pain and horror borne by the victims of this imaginary science.

Let us again direct our attention to the dog whose circulation is being studied. The string that forcibly pulled down the right hind-limb to a slit in the table, has got undone, and the leg regains its natural position, pushing away the cloths that covered the abdomen. There are no movements in the uplifted leg; it is stiff and motionless, as if it were part of a dead body. There is blood everywhere, on the floor, on the table, on the dog's paw, and on the hands of the vivisector, who goes on lecturing without minding the red colour on his hands. After some minutes the assistant demonstrator sees the escaped leg, and leisurely takes hold of the end of the string tied round the paw, pulls it down, and fixes it again to the table.

There are only a few spectators to-day, and the private research can begin almost at once when the lecture is concluded. A connection by means of a long glass tube is established between the crural and carotid arteries and the differences in blood-pressure noted.

The director of the laboratories is anxious to make the most of the dog, that is so quiet and nice to experiment upon, and he therefore proposes to test the action of betain, neurine, choline, and muscarine. It is especially the action of betain that he finds interesting, as he is inclined to think it poisonous. He declares that certainty in this respect is of great commercial importance, as it is closely connected with the production of beetroot sugar. The lecturer, however, does not at all share his opinion, and answers that he does not think there will be any effect at all on the dog, and that he is quite sure that the animal will not die of it. Twenty minutes more are spent in betain studies, and it is proved that it has no effect. It is very strange, therefore, to hear the director a few days later state in a lecture that he still thinks betain poisonous. Why is not a valuable experiment on an animal trusted?

An hour and a half have now been spent in work on this dog. The demonstrators have not told us that the dog has been anæsthetised, we have not seen any anæsthetic used during this long period, nor has there been any smell of ether or chloroform in the room.

When an anæsthetic or narcotic has been given to the animal, the students are told so, or they see the anæsthesia being kept up by repeated doses of the anæsthetising agent.

We conclude that the wonderfully quieting and completely satisfactory curare has immobilised this dog.

# A Grand Demonstration

*King's College*

MARCH 25TH, 1903

## A GRAND DEMONSTRATION

THERE is a strong smell of ether meeting us as we walk up the stairs leading to the physiological department. Medical students, qualified doctors, young men who hope to reach the minarets of independent physiological science, grey-haired men, with faces moulded frigid by years of private research, hurry into the lecture-room. The room is crowded by an animated audience. The professor of the laboratory introduces the lecturer, who is greeted by enthusiastic applause.

There are not less than three animals prepared for experiments: an Irish terrier, a white rabbit, and a tabby cat. There is no stinginess when an eminent man of science is going to impart his knowledge to others.

Pancreatic secretion is the subject of the lecture, and the animals have been fastened and cut up accordingly.

The animals are all in a row on their backs, the dog in the middle, the cat to the right, and the rabbit to the left. One laboratory attendant is watching over the dog and the cat, another, a boy, is standing by the rabbit. Drops of ether are now and then poured on cloths laid over the heads of the animals. The dog and the rabbit are lying still; the cat struggles. The neck and the abdomen have been opened in each animal.

The lecturer refers to the work on the pancreas done by Claude Bernard, Heidenhain, and Pawlow. In speaking about the latter, who always worked with permanent fistulæ, the professor makes the important remark: "He always insisted on the necessity of perfect physiological conditions, that is, no pain and no anæsthesia."

He also speaks about the researches of Popielski, who showed that even after section of the vagi and extirpation of the ganglia, the introduction of acid into the duodenum produces flow of pancreatic juice. Wertheimer, in France, confirmed Popielski's theory.

Bayliss and Starling obtained just as good a flow of pancreatic juice when the solar plexus was extirpated. They, therefore, came to the conclusion that the secretion of pancreatic juice is not of nervous origin but of chemical.

The experiments about to be made are intended to show the correctness of this view, and the lecturer says that he is sure his audience will like better to see the actual experiments than only to listen to his account of them, although the success of demonstration experiments always is uncertain.

He begins with the dog, by injecting twenty cc. of hydrochloric acid into the duodenum. The flow of pancreatic juice is expected to be greatly increased, but the expected effect does not appear.

"For this experiment it is best to use a dog in a starved condition," says the lecturer; "this one, however, came in only recently, and his pancreatic juice has been secreted in digestion."

From where did the dog come? Who brought him there without having the sense to starve him beforehand?

The reason, then, of the failure of this first experiment was that the dog had not been kept long enough within the precincts of the physiological laboratory. Some poor ignorant person had fed him—perhaps one who loved him, and perhaps one who had no idea of the fate the dog would meet with a few hours later. His master may have "lost" him early this morning, and perhaps in his ignorance of the needs of this scientific age, he now anxiously hopes for his return every minute.

But no advertisements and no rewards will bring this dog back, he is quite safe here.

The professor now cuts open the belly of the dog with a pair of scissors, ligatures vessels, and cuts out the duodenum. The blood streams down his hands and over the dog's body. He carries the

## A Grand Demonstration

piece of intestine to the water-tap, turns the tap, and cleans the duodenum. He then cuts it open, lays it on the table, and carefully scrapes off the interior mucous membrane. This is then put in a mortar and ground with powdered glass. Some acid is added. The mixture is heated in a bowl over a flame and stirred for about five minutes, then filtered.

The lecturer is now going to inject four cc. of this liquid, but before doing this he arranges the disordered parts of the mutilated belly. When doing this he explains that the mixture contains a depressor substance, and that he expects struggling will occur after the injection, and that "the dog's intestine might fall out" if care is not taken to keep it in place. This remark is fully appreciated by the audience, who applaud and laugh.

After the injection there is a good flow of pancreatic juice.

The operation-table with the dog is now carried to the side of the room, and the turn has come for the rabbit.

During the time that has passed the boy who is attending the rabbit has several times poured ether on the cloth over the rabbit's head. But in spite of that, the animal once stretched up its fore-limbs, which were not fixed to the table, and began to struggle.

When the table with the operation-board is now lifted up, and the rabbit carried to the place in the middle where the dog had been, the little animal again stretches up its fore-paws with claws thrust out.

The duodenum extract is now also injected into the rabbit. Violent struggling movements are produced, the animal lifts up its head, which is not tied down, and rises from its prostrate condition. The lecturer and the boy then hold it down.

The result on the pancreatic secretion of this injection is very slow in manifesting itself, and after a few minutes' waiting the professor declares that "it is not worth while to wait for this any longer. Let us try the cat"!

The rabbit on its board is then carried into a corner of the room. The lecturer

## A Grand Demonstration

tells us that we can look at it afterwards, and that the pancreas of a rabbit is very small, and that there is a continuous small flow of pancreatic juice in these animals, about one drop in every minute. After injection there ought to be two drops a minute. But he is almost sure that this experiment will be a failure.

The rabbit keeps moving its paws and will not leave off struggling. The professor of the laboratory tells the boy something and hands him the bottle of ether. The boy takes up the board with the rabbit, and walks out of the lecture-room with the rabbit in one hand and the bottle in another. When the animal cannot keep up a good appearance it had better go out of the room.

After a little while the boy returns with the bottle.

The cat is carried to the spot where the previous demonstrations have taken place. Ether has been administered to this animal once before the lecture began, and now another dose is given by one of the professors, after some words from the laboratory attendant. The cat has been struggling all the while whilst the dog and the rabbit were used, but it is lying still just now, because of the last dose.

The same extract is injected into the cat. The lever in connection with the pancreatic secretion shows a good flow.

"Cats differ from other animals in the extreme ease with which you get stoppage from the heart. We shall probably get a fall in blood-pressure and inhibition of heart. I hope it will not be permanent," says the lecturer.

Some pancreatic juice is now collected from the dog, mixed with starch and heated. After fifteen minutes we get "a lump of sugar, almost entirely maltose."

The professor concludes his lecture, amid applause, by repeating that the mechanism of the secretion of pancreatic juice is a chemical one, and says that this is the first instance we have of a chemical co-ordination.

Between twelve and a quarter to two the dog has had drops of ether sprinkled over the cloth over its head about five times. But at a quarter to two we see the dog, which hitherto has been quiet, suddenly turn the head, which is not fixed in a head-holder, the shoulders, and the upper part of the back over to the left side, as much as the tied paws permit. The animal then begins to struggle. The professor of the laboratory sees this, and hastens to sprinkle some more ether over the cloth.

The spirit of vivisection has seized the spectators. They rush down to the animals; there is loud discussion of the theory that has been demonstrated.

When going out we meet the boy carrying the miserable white rabbit into the lecture-room again. The little creature lies still on its board, the head is wet, the hairs stick to the skin, the eyes are protruding and look like glass balls.

The boy is polite and steps aside to let us pass. There is a murmur of many voices from the lecture-room—debated questions are filling the souls of knowledge-seekers with new life, and scientific interest runs high. We have seen a demonstration of careful, complete, and public vivisectional anæsthesia as it is now practised. What about the careless, incomplete, and private?

**Vivisection Bankrupt**

# VIVISECTION BANKRUPT

"Perfect physiological conditions, that is, no pain and no anæsthesia" (*See page* 140).

No condemnation of the methods of present experimental physiology from the mouths of anti-vivisectionists could be more valuable to their cause than this description of perfect physiological conditions, given by one of the recognised leaders of the science. Pain and anæsthesia, indeed, make physiological conditions abnormal, and the conclusions drawn from experiments under such conditions erroneous, whenever they are used to build up a science of physiology instead of one of experimental animal pathology.

Scientific opponents of vivisection have always based part of their objections to its practice on this simple and indisputable fact, and it is therefore a matter of no small importance to them to hear this admission from a vivisector.

When we enter the physiological laboratories, wherever they are and to whatever school they belong, what do we see?

In the stables and cages where various animals await their fate there is misery and half-conscious terror of the things of which they have a presentiment; when we follow them on their weary way up to the rooms where the operation-table, the knives and scissors, the electrical apparatus are ready for them, their mental anguish is soon augmented by bodily pain.

In the pain-tortured bodies, trembling under the sharp steel, bathing in their own blood, and in vain trying to tear the straps that fasten them to their crosses of agony, twitching under the piercing currents of artificial electricity, there is no trace left of the normal life in the nerves, in the blood, in the wonderful co-ordinated mechanism of the internal organs.

Or, when the nervous system, with its

myriads of delicate cells, the powers and innermost functions of which offer such unsolvable mysteries to our outer senses, is injured by curare, morphia, ether, or chloroform, how can we under such conditions get the faintest idea of their true nature?

*Vivisection is bankrupt;* all the teachings and bloodstained theories which are brought out from these laboratories under the name of physiology make one stupendous fraud. When the day of a true science has reached its zenith they will disappear like the evil smoke which obstructed the dawn of morning after the revelling nights of sacrificial worship of infernal powers.

When visiting the Pasteur Institute in Paris some years ago, the kinship of the modern science of tormenting to the worst forms of immorality in the "dark ages" became painfully clear to us. The light of the much-praised nineteenth-century civilisation seemed far away in this palace of artificial disease and well-paid quackery, among the thousands of dying and dead (for the dead animals lay among the living in many cages) rabbits and guinea-pigs moaning under the burden of all kinds of human diseases.

After much scientific work and careful study we can reproduce our diseases in defenceless animals, but we cannot cleanse ourselves from them. Vivisection is bankrupt.

We saw the rabid dogs, whose brains had been poisoned and in whose eyes there was the look of despair. One little puppy stretched out a paw to us through the bars of the cage and looked up with a pair of appealing eyes.

We also saw the magnificent sepulchre of the "great Pasteur."

Mad dogs are dangerous, but this danger is nothing compared with that arising from the moral insanity of legally protected animal torturers.

Not until physiology and medicine cease to look for knowledge and healing in the bodies of injured animals can they penetrate into the region of the true and the healthy.

It happens sometimes that a vivisector

for a moment sees the bluntness of his knife.

Some time ago we heard a physiologist say: "We have only recently learnt the exact movements in the small intestine. If we expose the intestine of an animal the operation prevents good results. It is best studied with the Röntgen Rays."

But, on the whole, the present race of physiologists do not at all see the fallacy of working under imperfect physiological conditions.

# Anæsthesia

## ANÆSTHESIA

The effect of the various anæsthetics on animals is quite different from that on man. There is a great dissimilarity in the way in which different kinds of animals "take" anæsthetics. Moreover, one dog may become anæsthetised by a dose which does not affect another dog of the same size.

To be able fully to anæsthetise an animal requires patience and care. Our experience of vivisectional methods has taught us that whenever these are displayed, they are induced partly by anxiety to keep up appearances, partly by fear that the animal may die of the effect of the anæsthetic, and thus spoil the experiment.

We have never seen any signs of anxiety in the experimenters for the sufferings of the animals, nor have we heard them express any such consideration.

The improvements in animal-holders seem to be much more appreciated by vivisectors than the advancements in the art of giving anæsthetics.

On the previous pages we have given examples of experiments performed under various kinds of anæsthetics.

In the four experiments on dogs and cats on pages 19, 37, 67, 109, and in the experiment on a dog on p. 129, we have the right to infer that no anæsthetics had been given, altogether apart from the other indications that these animals were not under anæsthesia. If an anæsthetic is administered, it is the duty of every teacher of physiology, who performs experiments before a class of students, to let the class know this, and what kind of anæsthetic has been given, if it is not administered in their presence. It would be extremely unscientific not to do this, as the anæsthetic has a great effect on the condition of the animal, and the cognisance of the administration of the anæsthetic is therefore most essential to the student's accurate understanding of the experiments. This information is also, as we have described, given when an anæsthetic has been administered.

One of the experiments on dogs (that described on p. 55) was performed under morphia alone, which is not an anæsthetic, and under which, according to Claude Bernard, "the animal remains sensitive; a touch on the cornea induces the closing of the eyelids; but he lies quite still, and lends himself without a movement to the most delicate operation; . . . he feels the pain, but has lost the idea of self-defence."

In another experiment on the brain of a dog morphia had been given and "scarcely any anæsthetic." Here we saw the animal open and shut its eye, which confirms the statement by Mr. J. A. W. Dollar in " The Practice of Veterinary Surgery," that " morphia is uncertain as an anæsthetic."

Several of the experiments described have been made under "morphia and a little chloroform"; in one of them (on p. 91) it was made clear that the anæsthetic and narcotic given had been equally inefficacious.

The period of anæsthesia produced by chloroform in the dog and cat is short, according to the veterinary expert just quoted. In the *British Medical Journal* of January 14th, 1899, p. 94, it is said that "Morphia does not act as a narcotic in dogs, but as a stimulant, large doses causing excitement."

We have also seen that ether, even after ostentatious and careful administration, does not always protect the animals from feeling pain.

What are the signs of pain, and when is an animal anæsthetised? In a curarised animal (like the dog described on p. 67) the signs of pain are suppressed, though the sensitiveness remains unimpaired.

Many vivisectors state that struggles do not necessarily indicate pain. Dr. G. W. Crile ought to be an authority on this subject; in describing experiment cxxxiii. in "Surgical Shock" on a fox terrier, he says: "In the control experiments, as well as in this, the dog was not under full anæsthesia. In the former the animal struggled on application of the flame." Dr. Crile rightly thinks that full anæsthesia is not accompanied by struggles. In complete anæsthesia all "reflex" acts have disappeared, all muscular movement is suppressed, and the eyeballs can be touched without causing blinking.

A struggling animal is never fully anæsthetised.[1] In a lecture on "The Action of Anæsthetics and Narcotics," the lecturer, who demonstrated the action of chloroform on a frog, told us that "the frog was anæsthetised, though not fully, for it responded to stimulation." In the greater part of the vivisectional experiments which we have witnessed, struggling has occurred, and the animals have indeed "responded to stimulation."

Severe operations on human beings are not performed when the patients are under "incomplete anæsthesia" (except in rare cases where it is previously known that full

[1] This is confirmed by Sir Benjamin Ward Richardson in "Biological Experimentation," where he says: " . . . when a deeply narcotised animal, under experiment, began to show the signs of movement indicating recovery from the narcotism."

anæsthesia would be dangerous to the life of the patient), and there is no elaborate apparatus for muzzling patients and keeping them fixed to the operation-table.

Dogs are much less susceptible to anæsthetics than rabbits. "In a rabbit the nerve-cells, especially of the cerebrum, show changes even after half an hour's anæsthesia, but in dogs at least four hours' anæsthesia must be employed ("On the Chemical Side of Nervous Activity," by W. D. Halliburton, M.D.).

Cats are said to be very susceptible to the action of anæsthetics, but sometimes they prove to be quite the reverse.

The kind of anæsthesia now produced in vivisected animals is, we fear, "more a curse than a blessing," and it is not necessary to remain long within the physiological laboratory to find out how splendidly it narcotises the public conscience.

# Frogology

# FROGOLOGY

All animals in the laboratory are handled like pieces of wood or clay, but the idea that frogs are sentient beings seems to be entirely absent.

"A fresh piece of skin," "a fresh nerve," or "a fresh heart" may be called for many times during an hour, and the required properties of some unfortunate frogs are fetched as readily as a little cotton wool or a piece of chalk. The essential experiments which have to be made by every aspiring student of physiology are, indeed, so firmly based on the existence of the frog, that one might feel inclined to call the first chapters of the science—"Frogology."

A look into any of the current physiological textbooks and handbooks for students will prove beyond doubt to the interested enquirer that the vivisector who flippantly termed frogs "God's gift to physiologists" had reason, from *his* point of view, to be grateful. "What does not humanity owe to that paragon of animals from a physiological point of view!" exclaims Professor Stirling in his "Apostles of Physiology," and then follows a eulogy on the usefulness of the frog. "Preparation of a frog's muscle," "a single contraction of a frog's muscle," "production of tetanus in a frog's muscle," "examination of the frog's heart," "the action of heat and cold upon the frog's heart," "the nerves of the frog's heart, and their functions," "action of drugs upon the frog's heart," "the effect of muscarine, atropine, and nicotine upon the frog's heart," "the effect of tetanisation of the vagus in the frog," "stimulation of the sympathetic in the frog," etc., etc., are some of the portals through which the neophyte in experimental physiology must wander, before he attains to the shrine where creatures of a higher order are sacrificed to the idol of knowledge.

It is commonly and thoughtlessly believed

that frogs feel very little, and among ten people who would be shocked at a cruelty practised on a cat, we should perhaps find only one who would be aroused to pity if a similar cruelty were practised on a frog. There is a kind of vague idea in the minds of the general public that frogs are used to a great extent for scientific experiments, and, when slightly acquainted with the vivisection controversy, many content themselves without further enquiry with the belief that the matter begins and ends with frogs. The unsympathetic attitude towards frogs has been much strengthened by the assertions of physiologists that most of the frogs experimented upon have had their brains destroyed previously, and that brainless frogs do not feel any pain. This statement is readily accepted by the unsophisticated, who are sure that they would not feel any pain if they were deprived of their brains, and who infer that it must be the same with all other creatures in the universe. The unbiassed enquirer will, to his astonishment, find that the scientific argument is indifferently built on very much the same kind of analogy.

The theory of *reflex* action, as contrasted with *automatic* action, has been largely studied upon frogs, and has lured many a mind away from the verdict of common sense in this matter. By reflex action is meant a muscular movement which is the response to an external stimulus. "Speaking popularly," writes Sir Victor Horsley in "The Structure and Functions of the Brain and Spinal Cord," "by the term reflex action is to be understood simply the fact that the nervous system provides the necessary apparatus to enable an animal to make response in the shape of a movement when it receives a sensory impression."

The A B C of reflex action is studied upon the spinal cord of the frog. The brain of a frog is destroyed, but *the spinal cord is left intact*. The frog is now subjected to different kinds of stimuli, and the animal's efforts to avoid these are considered as being typical instances of reflex movements. One of the toes of the left foot is pinched, the left leg is drawn up. A toe of the right foot is pinched, the right leg is drawn up. The skin of the flank is pinched, the leg of the same side is drawn up to push away the stimulus. One of the toes is touched with a heated wire, the foot is withdrawn. One of the feet is allowed to to be immersed in dilute sulphuric or acetic acid; in a short time the foot is withdrawn. Small pieces of paper dipped in acetic acid may be placed on different parts of the body, and the result will be different movements, which all tend to remove the irritant. If the right leg be held whilst the flank of the right side is irritated, the left limb will be drawn up in order to thrust away the irritating object. The animal is poisoned with strychnine: the slightest stimulus applied to any part of the animal will now produce violent tetanic spasms of the whole body. The poison has acted upon the spinal cord so as to produce what is called irradiation of reflex movements.

Physiologists admit that these movements are "complicated, co-ordinated, and purposeful in character,"[1] and that the muscular response is "in no way an irregular series of twitches of the limb muscles, but is a movement similar in nature to those carried out by the frog during its life, and that, when examined, it is seen to tend either to remove the irritating body, to move that part of the body from the irritant, or to remove the whole body."[2]

But in what way do these movements, which are *similar in nature to those carried out by the frog during its life*, differ from those which, under the same circumstances, would be produced in an intact frog? In no way at all. It is true that in an intact frog volition would not have been interfered with, and the animal would be capable of much more complicated efforts in order to escape. But the very fact that a brainless frog can make these "similar" and "purposeful" movements proves that the brain,

---

[1] "Elementary Practical Physiology and Histology," by M. Foster, M.D., F.R.S., and J. N. Langley, M.A., F.R.S.
[2] "Essentials of Experimental Physiology," by T. G. Brodie, M.D.

although already the "centre on the top of the centres," does not play the same part in maintaining consciousness in the frog as in the higher animals and in man.

In the higher animals these reflexes are not obtained, and it is found that the more complex the cord, the simpler are the "reflex movements." In dogs, cats, monkeys, and in man there are just a few movements which are classified as reflexes *of this kind.*

But on the whole the science of physiology contains no chapter where uncertainty, want of logic, and clear definition are more dominant than in that of reflex movements. You want to know whether a reflex movement is necessarily unconscious or not, whether pain can be a factor in the production of "reflex movement," and, if so, whether brainless frogs feel pain. You search the whole literature on the subject, from Whytt, Marshall Hall, and Pflüger down to the latest treatises, and you find yourself in a labyrinth of empty words and of vague ideas, and you also discover that not one thing, but at least ten different vital phenomena go under the name of "reflex action." We have heard a physiologist who lectured on reflex action classify the withdrawal of the foot of a brainless frog when touched with a heated wire, the withdrawal of the human foot when it is tickled, walking, manual skill, and—violin-playing as instances of perfect reflex action.

But for the present we are not concerned with this general muddle—one book would not be sufficient to describe that—and we leave it to the reflex violin-player to prove the difference between his art and the movements of a brainless frog.

When vivisectors shall be called upon to answer for their cruel actions, they will perhaps defend themselves by saying that all their skilful operations have been "pure reflexes."

What is of special interest to us now is to know whether the innumerable frogs experimented upon day by day by students taking their first faltering steps into the field of physiology suffer pain or not.

A great many frogs experimented upon

in the laboratories are *pithed*, *i.e.*, the cerebral hemispheres, the medulla oblongata, and the spinal cord are destroyed. If this is done thoroughly the frog is no doubt incapable of feeling pain, and the complicated "reflex movements" have disappeared.

But a great number, if not the greatest, of frogs experimented upon have had only their brains destroyed; their sensory faculties are not impaired, and they do feel the pain inflicted on them. To say that these animals are "pithed" is at least a misapplication of the word. Anybody who opens a handbook for beginners in experimental physiology can make sure of the terrible nature of the experiments made on frogs, the spinal cords of which have been left intact. From Bernard's classical curare experiment there is a long series of severe mutilations, the interest of which would be spoilt if the spinal cord were destroyed.

The question whether these frogs feel pain or not is a most important one for anti-vivisectionists who do not care only to protect the higher animals.

When we turn to physiologists to get an answer to this question, we get no definite response. "There is some sort of consciousness, but really there is no consciousness," we have heard a celebrated physiologist say.

Sir Victor Horsley is quite irritated at the idea that some people have cared to discuss this matter. He writes ("The Structures and Functions of the Brain and Spinal Cord"): "A vast array of writers have discussed the question as to whether we are to regard the lower animals as possessing, as they say, consciousness, and from this have even proceeded to formulate ideas as to whether they have a soul; while, owing to the remarkable discoveries of physiologists about forty years ago as to the functional activity, exhibited by the spinal cord of a frog when separated entirely from the brain, an animated debate was actually excited as to whether the spinal cord possessed the attributes of the mind. Speculations of this kind, however, are only rendered possible by the unjustifiable application of a metaphysical terminology—

## Frogology

which was originally devised for the analysis of the mental aspect of the most highly complex structure, viz. the brain of man—to the consideration of the simplest reactions of protozoa, small masses of protoplasm; and I do not propose, therefore, to waste time upon them."

Thus the great Sir Victor superciliously and, we are bound to say, unscientifically passes by the small masses of protoplasm. *Very* small masses of nervous protoplasm may yet possess attributes which baffle the most highly complex structure of man, as, for instance, the wonderful intelligence and delicate sensitiveness exhibited by such animals as bees and ants.

Whether we call these attributes mental or not is not of great consequence, and the "metaphysical terminology" is not at all necessary. So much time is devoted to the tastes of the small but fashionable microbes, that it is indeed surprising that considerations for the feelings of the frog should be treated with such scorn and as waste of time.

There are some great scientists who do not despise the small frog quite so much as Sir Victor Horsley. Among them are M. Charles Richet, Professeur à la Faculté de Médicine, Paris. We quote the following, translated from his "Des Mouvements de la Grenouille Consécutifs à l'Excitation Electrique": "A careful examination of the animal will prove that there is a very great difference between the reflex movement, even if generalised, of a frog without medulla oblongata and the movements of defence and escape, prolonged and repeated, in an animal deprived of the cerebral hemispheres. Are we entitled to call the movements governed by the medulla oblongata voluntary? And if we call them reflex, ought we not to make a difference between them and the simple reflex movements executed by a frog without medulla oblongata?

"Can the movements of defence executed by a normal frog be described as reflex? I content myself with formulating these questions without attempting to answer them."

M. Charles Richet is not quite so sure as his brother scientists of the theory of frog reflexes.

A brainless frog can be made to jump, swim, croak, it will avoid obstacles, and turns over again when put on its back. If it is kept alive for some months it will recover part of the power which it has lost by the removal of its brain. The longer it lives, the more its condition resembles that of a normal frog, and at breeding-time brainless frogs obey the laws of Nature.[1]

Physiologists do not care to discuss whether these frogs, the movements of which are similar to those of living frogs, feel the vivisectional torture or not. But it is only logical to infer that as long as these purposeful and complicated "reflexes" occur, that is, as long as the spinal cord is left intact and the frog tries to defend itself against the injury inflicted, there is a conscious sensation of pain.

In a completely anæsthetised frog, or in a frog the spinal cord of which has been de-

[1] "Manipulations de Physiologie," par Léon Frédéricq.

stroyed, these movements and all purposeful efforts to escape are entirely abolished.

But the frog is not anæsthetised. When convenient it is immobilised; this, according to a renowned French teacher of physiology, can be done in various ways, as, for instance, by curare, hot water, fixing with pins, etc.

A great deal has lately been written on the cruelty of feeding snakes with live animals. Some time ago, when visiting the Zoological Gardens, we saw a living frog in the cage of the yellow cobra. The cobra was asleep, and the frog sat in a corner of the cage and stared at the snake, motionless with fear. Some hours later we saw another frog in a physiological laboratory. And we thought that that frog would by far have preferred to be in the cage of the yellow cobra.

# The School of Mercilessness

# THE SCHOOL OF MERCILESSNESS

THERE is something in vivisection which makes it abhorred by those who stand foremost morally and spiritually. The outcry against it grows stronger day by day, and just as a Tennyson, a Browning, a Wagner, and a Victor Hugo have felt a deep indignation and contempt for this inhuman practice, there are certain qualities in the character of every man who becomes a vivisector which have led him to take up this kind of " work," and which mark him off as an enemy of ethical progress.

No person of truly refined mind could be a vivisector. Those who volunteer into the army of vivisectors must feel no shame at inflicting pain on the small and the helpless.

What is the influence on the young students who attend vivisectional demonstrations? We do not hesitate to say that, as a rule, it is distinctly brutalising, that the majority of the students are tainted by the callousness towards the sufferings of the animals which is so clearly demonstrated by their seniors. Very often vivisection is received like a kind of entertainment; there is laughter and merriment, and nearly always there is evidence that most of the students find the proceedings extremely " exciting."

They do not reflect much on the moral side of the question. Medical students have to get on, and be in touch with the latest achievements of science. Those who seek honours or desire degrees in physiology, and who prepare for taking up private research, are deeply impressed with the magnificence of the elaborate apparatus of clever men, dumb animals, and costly instruments. They are filled with the latest theories and debated questions of the science; they pry into the exposed entrails of the animals, and are already preserved against any uncomfortable feelings of pity.

The school of mercilessness is certainly

no school of heroism. We once saw a young man who was most interested in a vivisection; he squeezed the exposed lungs of the dog as if they had been a kind of sponge; he touched as many interior parts as he could reach, and had assumed a lofty scientific mien. During another lecture a few days afterwards, the lecturer asked whether any of the students would be good enough to allow him to demonstrate a little experiment with electrical currents on one of them. No one in the class answered. The lecturer then turned to one of them, which happened to be the young man so bold and scientific the other day, and said: " Will you let me demonstrate this on you?" The young man grew very pale and stammered something. " It is not at all painful," said the lecturer. The young man still hesitated, and looked as if he thought science the most foolish thing in the world. We could not help laughing, a few more joined us, and so the young man, after having been reassured that it was not painful, unwillingly went through his ordeal.

The effect on the laboratory attendants must of necessity be most debasing. We have seen some specimens of these in London and elsewhere, on whose faces the demoralising influence of perpetually witnessing and assisting in acts of cruelty has been clearly marked. Young boys employed in these laboratories are especially to be pitied. For what can they learn there that will help them to become good and unselfish men?

It is degrading for a man to spend a life in acts of cruelty, but it is ten times more so for a woman.

"But surely," people will ask, "*women* cannot approve of vivisection?"

We fear they can and do. Many anti-vivisectionists had hoped that medical and scientific women would work actively to abolish this form of research; but, on the whole, they have been found to put their humane feelings aside, and to accept without protest the scientific gospel of torture.

The woman-vivisector has arrived. She "works" with perfect tranquillity, and is above all anxious to blot out sentiment.

Girls who study medicine, and who do not themselves vivisect or attend vivisections, have all the same to listen hour after hour, week by week, to the details of physiological experiments of the most repulsive kind. There is no other physiology for them; they are taught by clever scientists who disregard any physiology not based on cruelty to animals. They get used to vivisection and to the " necessity " of it.

Even admirers of vivisection may hesitate before the threatening increase in the number of vivisecting women. What a future we have to look forward to!

Will women who have been trained at the vivisection-table become gentle, loving mothers?

# An Exact Science

# AN EXACT SCIENCE

Some gleanings from our physiological notes:

"Although we find this in our textbooks, there is not the slightest evidence that it is true.

"One can never tell till one has stimulated what is going to happen. The effects are very uncertain.

"That experiment, however, requires further repetition and confirmation in the light of our present knowledge.

"Men of good and established reputation have here come to diametrically opposite results.

"They of course came to different conclusions.

"It is of course varying with the authority which describes it.

"It has a very different effect in different animals.

"In those experiments we are using very strong stimulation. So that the conditions are not at all normal.

"The question is at present in a very unsatisfactory state.

"But we must remember that no observations made on the brain when the skull is opened can be applied to the brain under normal conditions.

"Nearly all the observations made have taken place under abnormal conditions, and are consequently not correct.

"Before you can succeed in isolating the brain from all outer structures, the animal dies.

"The electrical excitation must of course be a very abnormal form of producing these results.

"This point must be of a fundamental importance, but we have yet no knowledge upon this subject.

"We must study this subject in the monkey or in man. It is of no use to study it in an animal like the dog, because it can never be compared with man.

"The inner surface of the heart is very sensitive, the outer insensible to touch.

"Introducing a cardiac sound in the heart of a horse. No pain whatever (!)

"Made on unanæsthetised horses, so that the conditions were normal.

"All these speculations with regard to the inner work in the muscles are more or less uncertain, but we have to go on till we find some that suit all our experiences in the laboratory.

"We cannot reproduce the actual conditions in life.

"This is one of the many disputed physiological points."

# Where do the Animals come from?

## WHERE DO THE ANIMALS COME FROM?

WHO brought the dog, that is fixed to the operation-table ready for the vivisection, to the laboratory? Who sold him to the tormentors for thirty pieces of copper?

Think of the weary days and hours spent in vain howling and crying for freedom before the horrible experiments begin. Think of the terror he must endure, tended by the merciless attendants of vivisection. Perhaps he has had a happy home and known nothing but kindness all his life—to-day there is only the rack and the knife for him. He can do nothing to ward off his terrible fate. He is now nothing more than some kilos of dog-flesh, purchased for the needs of the inferno of animals.

Owners of dogs and cats ought to pay attention to the revelations of how the living laboratory-material is procured, now and then published in the press. The Constantinople vivisector has no difficulty at all in finding his canine material, which he returns to the street, tortured but still alive, when he has done with it. From Germany and France there are many true stories of how cats and dogs have been stolen for the purposes of vivisection. The recent scandal in Chicago over the many dogs stolen and sold to the University, where they were found by their anxious owners who had succeeded in getting legal permission to search for their lost pets, throws light upon the supply of animals for scientific torture.

We have heard two students, studying physiology, discuss the efficacy of a cat-trap belonging to one of them.

Every lover of animals who enquires into the number of lost cats and dogs in London must be alarmed. The homes for these animals are doing excellent work in withholding a great many from the most terrible fate of all; but in spite of that, we are convinced that hundreds of lost animals find no other home than the vivisector's torture-trough. It has lately been discovered that the police in Oxford sell stray dogs to vivisectors, and we have not been reassured that the London police do not do the same. On December 18th, 1902, Mr. J. G. Weir, M.P., asked some questions in the House of Commons as to the methods of the police in dealing with lost and stolen dogs. In a communication of January 14th, 1903, from the Secretary of State to Mr. Weir (published in the *Zoophilist* of February 2nd, 1903) it is stated that :

"In the case of stray dogs the proceeds of any sale by the police are authorised by Sec. 18 of the Metropolitan Streets Act, 1867, to be carried to the credit of the Police Fund.

"The Secretary of State has considered, in consultation with the Commissioner of Police, your suggestion that dogs held by the police in connection with a charge of theft should be sent to the Dogs' Home at Battersea, but he regrets that this does not appear to be practicable.

"As regards the possibility that dogs sold by the police may be used for the purposes of vivisection, I am to point out that the statutes authorising the sale do not lay down any restrictions as to the persons by whom, or the purposes for which, the dogs may be bought, nor do they empower the Secretary of State to do so, and he does not think that it lies with him to attempt to go further than the law in this matter."

There is, therefore, not the slightest guarantee that the police are not rendering service to science at the same time as to the Police Fund.

Rabbits and guinea-pigs can be bought only too easily; in many places they are reared and fed on a large scale, for the sole purpose of being experimented upon.

The Moloch of vivisection is voracious; he is not satisfied with a few victims. Many people who carelessly lose their animals, or who thoughtlessly pass by lost dogs and cats in the streets, believing that a policeman or somebody else will take care of them, would not leave the little miserable strays unaided, if they had just once been inside the scientific chambers of horrors.

# The Barren Tree

# THE BARREN TREE

ARE any of the experiments which we have witnessed likely to alleviate the sufferings of mankind? We put this question to those who imagine that some good to humanity will one day arise from the darkness of the laboratories of vivisection, and make the world healthier and better.

There is not even the slightest pretence that experiments like these are made to further medicine; they are the offspring of science *pur et simple*, and their makers scorn the idea of any bondage to the healing art. It is now long ago since they declared that their science was a *distinct* science, and that they had the same right to pursue it without any claims to immediate utility as has the astronomer, the geologist, and the physicist.

It is "knowledge" they seek, and the only

knowledge which they value is bought by tormenting the sub-human races.

Their science is like a distorting mirror, where the fair face of Nature is changed into a series of hideous contortions.

They often talk as if the monopoly of absolute accuracy and perfectly correct representation of facts of necessity had been given to them because of their strictly experimental methods. But when we scrutinise the grand castle of their science we find that it rests on no solid ground, and that parts of it are continually falling to pieces and built up again on the same slough of deception.

The unsatisfactory state of the science is sometimes frankly admitted, though no other path is seen than more experiments on animals. In the preface to the " The Physiologist's Notebook," a summary of the present state of physiological science, for the use of students, by Alex. Hill, M.A., M.D. (London, 1893), we read: " The Notebook deals with the arguments of physiology, for it is as well that the student should, from the outset, recognise that the subject, although it has made rapid strides during the last twenty years, is still in an immature and transitional state, and that many most important issues can only be summed up as leaving a balance of evidence on the one side or the other—a balance which subsequent investigation may possibly disturb."

As long as the science is built on torture of animals it will remain in an "immature and transitional state." It does not aspire to the higher regions of thought, and the words of Huxley ("Life of Hume") seem singularly inappropriate: "The laboratory is the forecourt of the temple of Philosophy, and whoso has not offered sacrifices and undergone purification there has little chance of admission into the sanctuary." For whatever vivisectors are, they are not philosophers, and the vulgar atheism engendered in their laboratories does not prepare them for the temple of Philosophy.

They have to create a new and spiritualised vitalism before they can grasp any vital phenomena, for, as Dr. Lionel Beale writes in his "Vitality," "We are not machines, we are not governed by, or the results of, chemical and mechanical changes. Our life is not the mere outcome of chemical and mechanical forces." And the old investigators, who spoke about the undefinable spirit of life, were much nearer the truth and the sanctuary of lasting and sacred thought than the modern sellers and buyers of theories, based on matter, and matter only, and baptised in the blood of agony.

The experiments which have been described in this little book are only instances of one part of the appallingly extensive system of exposing the sub-human races to torture for the sake of a "knowledge" that debases the intellect, and a medical science that thinks that the body can be kept alive by killing the soul.

For the sake of the innocently tormented, for the sake of the unborn human race going to receive this cursed heritage, for the sake of the great belief in a life everlasting of mercy and love, this infamous practice must be put an end to.

PRINTED BY
HAZELL, WATSON AND VINEY, LD.,
LONDON AND AYLESBURY.